Wholesale Real Estate

The Fastest Way to Learn to be an Expert Real Estate Investor using Real Estate Wholesaling and Leveraging Other People's Money for Deals

By

Income Mastery

her competence. There are no scenarios in which the publisher or author of this book can be held responsible for any difficulties or damages that may occur to them after using the information presented here.

In addition, the information on the following pages is intended for informational purposes only and should therefore be regarded as universal. As befits its nature, it is presented without warranty with respect to its prolonged validity or provisional quality. The trademarks mentioned are made without written consent and can in no way be considered as sponsorship of the same.

Table of Contents

Introduction

The following article will address the issue of real estate in the United States. What we are going to look for is to inform whoever is interested in investing in the North American real estate sector so that they can resolve all their doubts and make the right decision according to their requirements and personal interests.

First, for those who want to secure their future and invest in the long term to grow their wealth, investing in the United States becomes an attractive possibility. "According to the world's leading real estate investors, the U.S. continues to lead the ranking as the most stable and secure country for real estate investment and capital appreciation opportunities. (Ambito .com)

A survey conducted by the Association of Foreign Real Estate Investors (AFIRE) showed that 95% of its members will maintain or increase their investment in the United States.

According to this, the following article is going to be structured in a series of possible questions that can be asked by anyone interested in the world of real estate.

First, we are going to tackle the problem of why we have to invest in real estate and not in any other type of investment. It is hoped that the article will be able to resolve the initial doubts of any person interested in this sector and that they may have the dispensable tools to get started. Secondly, it is going to explain why investing in America is so good. This is especially due to the security of its economy and the stability of its currency.

Third, we will talk about how the process of investing in real estate works. Fourthly, it will explain how the real estate business is in the United States, which are the main real estate companies that can facilitate the work, advise and accompany in all the legal proceedings to the person interested in real estate.

Fifthly, there will be a small list of the conditions that an investor needs to be able to invest in real estate. Special emphasis is placed on the case where the interested party is a foreigner, although it also includes those who have U.S. residence or nationality. Sixth, it details the three best places to invest in the United States. It details the pros and cons, the reasons why they became interesting areas for the real estate sector, as well as the average prices per square meter (^{m2}).

Seventh, they will offer a series of platforms to be able to invest with little money. This allows those who want to start in the real estate market to do so with little cost, driven by the money of others, with short-term income and safely. In this section we will also detail the pros, cons, recommended options and some other indispensable advice before getting fully involved in the investment.

Eighth, in order to position the reader in a current context, a series of important news found in 2019 on the real estate market is detailed. The most important thing is to highlight the problem that the real estate sectors are facing in the face of climate change, the strong hurricanes that collide with the North American coast and the constant rise in sea level. These are all factors that impact the decision making of those who wish to invest in order to obtain long-term income and thus avoid future losses of money due to natural disasters, events that human beings cannot easily control.

Finally, a conclusion of the article is presented, detailing the conclusions to which this research led and a kind of summary so that the reader can decide and know what steps to take in order to start investing in real estate in the United States.

It is essential that the client first considers their interests and resources in order to invest in the United States. If you require additional information, we suggest you to consult a specialist in the real estate market, as well as in the North American tax sector, in order to be able to answer all the doubts that may arise after reading the following work. It should be clarified that we are not specialists and that the purpose of this article is to be able to give to our readers a different perspective, so that they can know which places to go to or how to start the procedures to be able to own a property or invest in several properties.

Why Invest in Real Estate?

Many times, in the financial world there are certain risks that can help us to increase our assets. There are risks in investing in stocks and funds. In addition, the savings account usually contributes very little to be a source of investment. In a short time, whoever wants to use these options ends up paying a lot of taxes on investment risks. The solution in these cases is to invest in real estate. Even in times of economic and financial crisis, investment in real estate remains profitable. The value of the property's capital tends to increase in the long term and the property can provide income by renting it.

We are now going to give you different reasons arguing why investing in real estate is much better and safer than any other kind of investment.

1. Investing in real estate is much better than saving

The interest rates of savings accounts are not usually high and depending on each economic situation, often inflation beats that interest and ends up exceeding the return of that fixed term chosen. That's why, the best option is to invest in a property. With a good transaction the client will be able to see the increases of his capital, as well as monthly income by the rent of the same one. It could be said that even retirement would be assured in the long term.

2. Investing in real estate avoids the risks of weak currencies.

In times of crisis many national currencies are affected by turbulent events in weak economies. This means that due to devaluations of national currencies many end up being worth less than the Dollar or the Euro. The vast majority of properties are priced in dollars, to maintain a certain similarity with the regional or international market. This is why it is very important that investments, if the client lives in a country with an unstable economy, are in dollars. Thus, by investing in real estate you pass through the ups and downs of economic crises and keep your capital safe.

3. Investing in property generates extra income with an income

There are two benefits to having a rental property. First you can have your savings insured in brick value and second you can rent the property and generate fixed monthly income. The profitability of a property, annually on average, has a return of 7 or 8 percent.

4. Investing in real estate is much safer than investing in the stock market.

Investing in the stock market is not easy for anyone on the street. You require certain knowledge to be able to understand how the system is managed and what the risks are. Stock values all the time are fluctuating drastically and the financial sector all the time has new investment products: complex systems with minimal or uncertain returns. It is not in dispute that many times, in a short term, enormous profits are obtained and much faster than a rent. But the stock market is tied to economic crises, which makes the system very uncertain, something that long-term investment in the real estate sector does not have.

5. Investing in real estate says goodbye to unstable prices

Putting our savings into raw materials such as gold or silver is also risky, because their value is volatile, so their prices are very unstable. In recent years the price of gold and avocado fell abruptly. Because of this, financial specialists continue to assert that the best and most stable thing is to invest in brick.

6. Invest in real estate instead of investing in pension savings or insurance

Life insurance, pensions or group insurance are usually stable and reliable investments for the future. However, what really happens is that they are not oblivious to financial crises. Many times, banks or insurance companies are affected by these crises, leading them to have to close for bankruptcy. Moving to another company is often very expensive, leaving the client exposed to these situations. That is why the best thing is still to be able to invest in the real estate sector.

7. You do not only invest in real estate, but also in your retirement

Most workers know that the minimum salary of their retirement is not often enough or ends up suffering devaluations due to inflation in many countries. Also, with the possible failure of interim systems or welfare state due to increasing age of people and rising hopes. All of this is not very good for the retirement system, as it begins to collapse due to high demand and the small number of workers who support it. In short, there are many who receive retirement and very few who work to maintain that retirement system (this is also due to the decline in the birth rate of populations). All this is solved by investing, thinking about the future, thinking about having an additional income such as renting one or more properties.

8. How to invest in real estate at affordable prices? It's best to invest in well properties

The best thing in the economic market is to invest in funds because construction companies are often looking for investors who can help with construction costs. Even if you don't want to keep the property you can sell it at a higher price, getting a profit return compared to the initial price of the property in fund. You can then reinvest that earned money in another property with the same characteristics and so on.

9. Investing in property is fiscally profitable

On the other hand, investing in this real estate sector helps the tax declaration. This is because taxes are set on the indexed cadastral income of the property and not on the rental income (this according to each country's tax law). It is important that anyone interested on investing consult a specialist on tax law. Many times, the annual fees for maintaining properties are much lower than paying taxes on other types of income.

10. Keep your money in parking lots. Another type of real estate investment.

There is another investment market in the emerging real estate sector that is very stable. These are the garages and parking lots. Cars in big cities are used very little, more than 90% of the time they spend stored in a parking lot. Therefore, parking lots will always be required. These places are expected to increase over time, as the demand is growing steadily and the number of cars in cities tends to be greater than free parking spaces. For this reason, in the future, the values will be higher to rent the place and to buy it. Another key advantage of this real estate sector is that maintenance is much lower than a home.

Why is it so Attractive to Invest in the U.S.?

First, it is because the income is in dollars: the vast majority of investors will find it attractive to invest in real estate in this country because the income from the rents is in dollars. It should be made clear that not only is the dollar practically the currency of world trade, but it is also one of the most stable in the world. Because of this, many foreign investors see the possibility of maintaining and growing their wealth in this continent, especially if they come from emerging countries or countries with less economic stability.

Secondly, investment mechanisms are simple and easy. The United States, with the objective of attracting investment in its territory, facilitates and encourages foreign investment, and offers a predictable and transparent judicial system. The real estate market is very well regulated and has a lot of transparency since there is a public listing of the properties on the Internet, where the value of this, who is the owner and all its former owners.

Third, there is continuous economic growth and therefore the real estate market is reliable for investment and long-term profitability. Despite the crisis of 2008 with the bankruptcy of the Lenmann Brothers, the North American real estate sector is growing again. Although the values are reduced, in the long term they are going to recover and increase again. This is why investing now is the best decision you can make.

How does the investment process work?

There are companies, such as Prodigy Network, that accompany the client in the purchase process, give legal and tax advice and act as property managers. All this allows the investor to feel secure and be sure that the transaction will go well and create results.

Each company has its own mechanisms and its own rules. Some can provide security to the customer in terms of their annual returns. This is done by depositing the income from an agreed period into a trust account. This is because a large number of properties that were sold with pre-sale credit today are still unoccupied. Even so, North American house prices continue to drop throughout the country, except for New York. However, the states with the highest Latino demand are California, Texas and Florida.

Having a real estate broker allows the investor not only to obtain a good offer but also to ensure the rent and reduce risks. Therefore, companies advise investors in the search and choice of housing. All this based on the needs and criteria of the client. Then they go with you during the process of buying and fighting, like managing the opening of the bank account.

The company's fees vary. For example: Miami Tango charges a commission for the sale of the property and then establishes a management contract. At first, you are charged one month's rent and between 5% and 10% of the annual income, depending on the area of the property.

If you want to avoid the services of these real estate companies and want to go through all the process by your own, it is essential to consider and know in depth all the requirements that the government imposes to buy and sell in real estate as well as tax obligations. In addition, it is necessary to have the advice of a specialized lawyer. In summary, the requirements for foreigners are letters of reference from the country of origin (some bank) and a bank account opened in the country.

It will also require a local accountant who can certify the activity of the buyer and the way in which they will generate income and payment of the monthly mortgage -down payment- (which can range from 20% and 30% in residential areas and up to 40% in commercial areas).

What is the Real Estate Business like in the United States?

Firstly, in order to decide on the potential of the investment, four points must be assessed.

1. Rental values: this factor must be considered in order to evaluate the profitability and the expenses you are looking for while waiting for the value of the property to increase.

2. The average price of the property: it is indispensable to consider the average price, as well as the historical price to be able to consider the possibilities of valuation of the property.

3. Quantity of sales: it is also important to have studied the area and the number of constructions that are made in the area. This is because the customer or interested party can know and have a map of the dynamism of the market.

4. Finally, the local economy: the most important thing when investing in a house with a desire to rent is to know the state of the local economy. It is important that the city, area or state in which the focus is placed has an economic dynamism that is growing or booming. That guarantees local employment, stimulates local tourism or shows signs of budding economic growth.

Once the property in which you want to invest is found, before finalizing the operation, it is important to know the payment of taxes and the rules that change according to the migratory status of the buyer. If you generate the transaction as a foreign individual, or under other modalities, taxes can rise up to 40% for when you want to transfer it, give it as a gift, sale or inheritance it. That is why it is essential to consult with a lawyer specialized in real estate to clarify all doubts and also to advise you on the best way to get the property, reducing the battery of taxes that can arise.

There are different ways in which a foreigner can acquire a property. Some of these are: a corporation, a partnership, a limited liability company or co-ownership.

Julian Myers, an international lawyer, explains that "creating the perfect structure for a non-resident U.S. client is like making a custom-made suit. Their circumstances and objectives must be analyzed in order to find the best option for the specific needs of the client. While a certain structure may work for one client, it may be the worst option for another" (Forbes, 2019).

This is why it is very important that before carrying out any transaction of purchase and sale of real estate the interested party is advised with a group of experts to be able to clarify all the doubts and not to commit errors that in a future could affect the finances.

On the other hand, certain things must be considered to start the investment:

It is necessary to be conscious of the amount of money that will be allocated to the investment. It must also be taken for granted that it may be a long-term investment (two to five years) and that it cannot be liquid. Some experts explain that a million and a half pesos is an interesting amount to start investing, since a smaller amount reduces the options. On the other hand, in order to generate a capital gain, the investment must be allowed to mature within three or five years.

It should be clarified that the capital gain in a property depends on whether there may be a real estate project, which is planning the construction of important roads or which may become a fashionable area or with some commercial growth. All this a real estate advisor can find in the real estate market.

Factors to Consider when Investing in Real Estate

It is important that when you are going to invest in real estate, the property must be registered in the Public Registry of Property, know its fiscal situation, that it can be deeded, that it is legally processable -that is, that it has deeds-, that it is not intestate, that it can identify hidden vices of the property and that the area is known.

It is also important to note that 8% of the value of the property ends up in notary or tax expenses. Therefore, it is effective to approach a real estate specialist with a marked track record, since unfortunately anyone can buy or sell without previous experience or knowledge. A stockbroker or insurance intermediary requires a license to practice, a real estate advisor does not. Which could put the estate at risk.

Pre-sale: obtaining a pre-sale asset and then investing in high levels of capital gain is an attractive option. If you buy a project in a well or in a plan, it allows you to obtain a property at a lower price than what would come out after completing the project. But it is very important to consider the developer, researching at Profeco, visiting the offices or asking for recommendations.

After acquiring the property can be remodeled and increase its value and sell if desired, achieving profits of up to 30%. A great option is the San Rafael colony, which has very nice houses from the 30s and 40s.

What do I Need to be an Investor?

Vivi Celeita, a foreign sales specialist with Partnership Realty Inc. commented that the basic requirements for buying a home as a foreigner in Florida are:

> "To have tourist or resident visa; to give the initial quota of the property, valued between 20% and 30% of its total value; certificate of income by an accountant; and a letter signed by your financial entity that reflects and validates good credit management, which can be from your country". (The Republic, 2019)

Who qualifies to buy in the United States? It's a very simple answer that customers usually get when they start to have a lot of doubts before investing. The answer is very easy: any person or company that can prove that they have the income or what it takes to pay for the property they wish to acquire, either in cash or through financing, may be a potential buyer.

Is it possible to acquire financing from abroad? In case you want to obtain financing, not all banks have loans designed for foreigners. That's why it's best to contact an expert in these financings who can advise the interested party on U.S. real estate. This expert will not only offer different options that can be adapted to the client's needs at the time of wanting an economic loan but will also be present and facilitate the paperwork process necessary to apply for financing and increase the chances that the credit will be approved.

What visa or status is required to purchase property in the United States? It is also a very common doubt that has a very simple answer. Although you can buy properties with different immigration status, you can buy a property with a non-immigrant view, such as a tourist view. The indispensable thing to be able to carry out the transaction with this visa is to demonstrate that as a buyer you are solid and to be advised by an international lawyer who is an expert in taxes for foreigners.

How to start the process? The first thing to do is find a real estate expert in the city where you are interested in investing in real estate. It is important that you speak your native language, as this will facilitate communication in the process (for example, in this case I would recommend that you look for an agent who speaks Spanish). These experts are international and immigration lawyers, financial advisors, foreign financing experts, real estate advisors, etc.

Local rules for investing in the U.S. are an issue to keep in mind. The seller of a property must pay a tax on the difference earned between the purchase and the sale. On the other hand, now it is going to be sold, those who are foreigners, suffer a 15% withholding that after having filed the tax return is released. From then on, the payment is credited with the lien on the profit made. This whole process can take about a year. However, this

21

withholding does not occur if the property is in the name of a company.

In many U.S. states, a homebuyer does not pay the real estate commission, but the seller does. This commission is about 6% of the total value of the operation. On the other hand, inscription costs 2% of the value.

The Best Places to Invest in USA

Detroit: The Future Star of the Real Estate Sector

Those who know the American real estate business know that the best place to buy is Detroit.

> "This city, which reached the point of bankruptcy, began to resurface in 2013 when a group of businessmen led by Dan Gilbert decided to reconvert the trend and give the metropolis a new life. Today, big brands are establishing themselves there, from Nike to Starbucks," describes Marcelo Schamy, an Argentinean who has lived in the United States for more than three decades and CEO of IDG Home Detroit, a real estate investment company that has sold more than 700 houses and is making inroads into the purchase of complete office buildings, which are already in operation and with a tenant company with a current contract" (La Nación, 2018).

The city currently has prices below the country's average, which is why properties will be revalued in the coming years, as they are doing so at a rate of fifteen percent annually. The square meter is at 630 dollars, while in the rest of the country it is at 1500 dollars. The key, according to some agents steeped in the subject, is to invest in single-family homes, because they are easier to rent and have fewer expenses.

According to Eduardo Perez Orive, CEO of Properties in Detroit, as far as the areas are concerned, the East has the best geographic location: the most important neighborhoods are Morningside, East English Village and Harper Wood. For those who are interested in investing in this city, Properties in Detroit makes tours that leave Miami and during the day visit Grosse Pointe.

> "Other interesting places to invest are Midtown, the Cass Avenue corridor, Woodbridge and New Center. Its value lies in its demographics, its proximity to Wayne University, medical centers and downtown," adds Ariel Arrocha, director for the Argentina Business USA Law Firm" (La Nación, 2018).

In conclusion, Schamy says that the three reasons for investing in Detroit are population growth, employment growth and affordability of investments.

For many analysts and real estate specialists, over the next three to five years, Detroit's city values will grow twice as fast as they are today. In addition, the city guarantees great legal certainty, as in most cities in the United States.

Something similar to what happened in Miami in 2009 is happening in Detroit. After the 2008 crisis, prices rose, so a difference can be made. This city is located to the north of New York and limits with Canada. At its peak during the 1900s and 1950s it was considered the "Paris of the West" and was the fourth largest city in the USA. After the crisis of the automotive industry it became a ghost town.

However, by 2015 many entrepreneurs, corporations and officials came together to discuss the future of this beautiful city and decided to give it a new focus. That's why local businesses have been boosted, as well as retail stores and high-tech firms. Eventually great investors arrived such as Dan Gilbert (owner of the Cleveland Cavaliers team) with $1.8 billion, Slim and Warren Buffet. All this favored the development of employment that had died with the flight of the automakers in search of cost reduction and allowed local economic growth. All these variables are what make Detroit one of the most profitable options, since it maintains a distance between the prices per ^{m2} of other U.S. cities, but also shows a booming, sustained and attractive economic growth for real estate investors.

Miami: A Classic of the Classics

Florida is one of the most popular destinations due to the ease of finding Spanish speakers for those seeking to invest in the United States. In this case, priority is given to the areas closest to the beaches: Fort Lauderdale (Broward), Key Biscayne (Miami-Dade) and South Beach. Brickell, Wynwood and Midtown, among many others, are also new destinations of choice.

Depending on the areas, both residential and commercial, prices vary enormously. You can find properties valued at $100,000, as well as others valued at a few million dollars. However, the average price of properties in Miami is under $700,000 (The Pablo Hobernman Nation).

> "Mariano Capellino, CEO of INMSA, says that "the volume of transactions has been reduced in recent years and the inventory has grown significantly due to the entry of new units that have been completed. This means that the values have been corrected downwards since 2015, on average 10 per cent annually. This situation has occurred mainly in the area of Brickell, Downtown and, to a lesser extent, in the beach area where values have fallen by an average of 5 percent annually in the last 3 years" (La Nación, 2018).

On the other hand, Vanessa Grout, president of CMC Real Estate in Miami, explains that sales increased in the area since July 2018.

> "According to the Miami Dade County Realtors Association, real estate sales of over $1 million were up 21.5 percent in June. We at Brickell Flatiron have seen, for example, a significant rise in sales of penthouses after the World Cup" (La Nación, 2018).

The main attractions of Miami Dade are the different kinds of properties that can be found. From futuristic skyscrapers, office towers, hotels and luxury shopping malls.

> "Renata Calderaro, immigration lawyer and CEO of Calderaro Tyrrell Law Group, recommends that her clients "in the case of Central Florida, avoid the acquisition of condominiums and look instead for the value of new homes, because they do not have so many additional costs and once rented the return on investment is faster. Long-term valuation is key and lending facilities are also key" (La Nación, 2018).

In Miami the price per square meter depends on the type of property. Who seeks to invest in renting the property usually looks far from the beach, as the value of taxes is much lower than for a property near the coast? A clear example is the Homestead area, where the $m2$ can be averaged at 1506 dollars.

Although new destinations for investors are emerging, experts continue to point to Florida. The potential is continuously growing as a real estate market, as it is tied to the area's sustained job growth. All this favored real estate development in cities such as Tampa, Cape Coral and Orlando.

According to Forbes magazine, since the beginning of the year, the state of Florida has the largest number of cities offering an investment climate. 4 of the top 10 U.S. cities to invest in real estate in 2019 are in Florida.

Some of these cities analyzed by the Rentberry rental housing service in the United States:

1) Fort Lauderdale: average rent: US$1937 per month. Average price of a medium house: US$318.141.

It is one of the best places in Florida, and although the rental price is one of the most expensive in the state, the value of the homes remains on average. In addition, real estate experts believe that prices will increase in the coming years. An important piece of information for those who want to purchase goods and then rent them is that Fort Lauderdale is the city with the highest growth in employment in Florida, so soon there will be a great demand for rentals and sales.

2) Tampa (average rent: US$1,186 per month. Average price of a medium house: US$173,250

During 2018 Tampa was considered the second-best city for real estate investments in the USA. What's more, almost the entire Tampa Bay area is considered one of the best places to buy and rent. Matthew Nagy, a member of Graystone Acquisitions, explains that in recent years, Tampa has suffered a two-digit valuation above its prices.

3)   Jacksonville: average rent US$1,061 per month. The average median house is $163,755.

In Jacksonville the value of homes increases by about 9% each year. In addition, the city has a population increase of 5% and employment growth of 4% per year.

4)   Orlando: average rent: US$1,327 per month. Average price of a medium house US$183.548.

Orlando is another interesting option for real estate investors. Tops the list of ratings in the real estate market. In addition to a growing economy, it also has an increasing population and labor market. Due to the increase in the labor market and the population, there is an increase in the demand for housing, both for rent and for purchase. Orlando, above all, is a very active city that continues to attract tourists from all over the world, as well as having a fledgling reputation as a new business center.

5)   West Palm Beach: average rent: US$1,480 per month. Value of a median home US$250,784.

It is one of the best cities with beach to invest in rental housing. The local market is dynamic and is characterized by a great variety of real estate options: from houses with a high value due to their proximity to the sea, as others a little cheaper in the western area of the city. Prices and location are two factors that make

West Palm Beach a very attractive market to invest in real estate.

Finally, according to USA Today, other cities that have a market that can be boosted in terms of real estate are Pittsburgh (Pennsylvania), St. Cloud (Minnesota), Houston (Texas), Chicago (Illinois), Indianapolis (Indiana) and Kansas City (Missouri).

During 2018 there was a striking phenomenon throughout the United States. And it is that the sale of the houses during the month of December fell surprisingly. And Miami-Dade had the same trend. "Central Florida county experienced a 6.2% decline at the close of December last year, **according to** the Miami Realtors Association report" (Real Estate America, 2019).

The increase in interest rates and the limited supply of properties available in the real estate market, with prices below $400,000, were the factors that generated a setback in the Florida county market. However, it should be noted that sales in Miami-Dade continue to be much lower than the falls in the rest of the country, with the national average being 10.3% compared to the previous year.

Also, interest rates suffered slight movements that many analysts in the real estate sector believe had a negative impact on the sale of properties in 2018. However, these rates are expected to increase and translate into a recovery in sales.

On the other hand, another study shows that values are expected to drop in Miami-Dade homes, after so many years of uncontrolled increase. Only 18% of respondents say there will be an increase in property values in the area, compared to 44% in 2018.

63% of those who participated in the survey explain that the values will remain stable, so there will be no decrease in them (in 2018 14% established that there would be a stability of values). On the other hand, 16% of those surveyed consider that the values are going to fall.

"Lynda Fernandez, spokeswoman for the Miami Association of Realtors, said that although the total number of home and condominium sales in Miami-Dade dropped 6.1 percent year-over-year in June, from 2,594 to 2,436, prices continued to rise. The average price of single-family homes rose 4.2 percent in June, from \$355,000 to \$370,000, while the average price of existing condominiums grew 4.2 percent, from \$240,000 to \$250,000" (The New Herald, 2019).

"While our condominium market is still affected by the limited availability of [Federal Housing Administration loans], we have seen price growth year after year in five of the last six months," Fernandez said. "Home prices have risen consecutively since 2011, during 91 months of successive increases. The market for single-family homes is balanced between buyers and sellers but is closer to the seller market. Based on current market behavior, we expect price growth to remain below five percent for both types of properties" (The New Herald, 2019).

Sixty-five percent of survey respondents think the current inventory value of properties, valued at $1 million, is a fair price, compared to 47% who say the value is exaggerated. On the other hand, in April, property values fell from 32 to 35 of the largest U.S. real estate markets, including Miami. All these factors analyzed by the survey show that everything that made home prices so high that it was impossible for local residents to buy them is likely to begin to decline.

"With the level of new luxury residential construction that Miami-Dade has enjoyed for the past three decades, I believe that our homes and condominiums currently offered for sale today could easily constitute the best quality luxury inventory of any major market in the world," said Ron Shuffield, CEO of Berkshire Hathaway HomeServices EWM Realty. "(The New Herald, 2019).

Shuffield explained that 25% of the single-family homes available in Miami Dade through June 30, 2019, offered by the Multiple Listing Service and valued at more than $1 million, are less than 10 years old. In addition, 43 percent of luxury condominiums with new construction have a similar rank.

"During the quarter ending June 2019, the average final sale price for a single-family home worth more than $1 million was 81 percent of the initial asking price, compared to 87 percent for the same period last year," Shuffield said. "The reduction in the average price of a luxury condominium, from its original list price to its final sale price, registered a 6 percent decrease, reaching 82 percent during the quarter ending June 30, 2019. (The New Herald, 2019).

Manhattan

Manhattan is seeing an unparalleled process that any investor will want to take advantage of. And the prices are going down. The square meter is at 1700 dollars, so it is an ideal opportunity for those who want to invest. Not only for those looking for condominiums, but also development projects (well) as there are many options in the area.

"This market was always the dream for the real estate investor, although unfortunately few arrive for the high value of the square meter and the reduced and scarce inventory suitable for the investor. Something that seemed unattainable today is possible through crowdfunding, where the investor can enter from U$S50.000 with profitability of two figures", clarifies Gonzalo Basaldua, co-founder of B&B Brokers". (La Nación, 2018)

Finally, an interesting fact is that, in New York, between 53rd and 59th Street, a new area valued in m^2 at 10,000 dollars is growing.

Brooklyn vs Manhattan

Many real estate investors prefer to invest in Brooklyn. This neighborhood is one of the most modern office markets in New York. It even allowed the city to position itself on the list of candidates to host Amazon's headquarters. Now New York can become another landmark in the real estate district.

According to an annual ranking by PwC and Urban Land Institute, Brooklyn became one of the most desirable markets in North America to invest in housing or commercial offices. According to this ranking it entered the top 10 for the first time in the last 40 years and this was achieved due to its industrial attractiveness and lower costs with respect to Manhattan, located in the 32nd position.

How to Invest with Little Money?

It's true that trying to invest in real estate has always seemed like something exclusive, requiring a lot of money. But it's not like that anymore. New technologies allow you to invest in real estate with little money and in a simple way. The article will present four ways to invest in real estate with little money and without having to leave the house.

1)   Crowdfunding real estate equity

In a real estate crowdfunding of equity type what can be done is that, several investors invest together in an apartment that, according to the behavior of the market, is expected to increase its value in a certain time. In other words, many people put money in something and between all of them they buy the apartment in pre-sale to be able to sell it in a near term.

Some applications that allow you to do that are:

- **M2CROWD**: where the investments are among the best because they have quite high yields, with low amounts and a lot of security.

- **Inverspot**: investing in this application is more complicated than in the previous one since the minimum amounts are higher, and it is not certain when they will be obtained as a profit or how long the investment will last. It is much more uncertain than M2CROWD and less recommended.

- **PM2**: real estate investments with this application are low amounts. However, they have few opportunities to diversify, and many times it is not even possible to diversify.

With these "community" investments it is necessary to recognize the following items:

- **Taxes**: not all applications withhold taxes equally, so it is essential to keep in mind the following: how much will they withhold? to know if they give receipts or invoices about this withholding. Many times, tax withholding is 20% of the return on the investment, but it is key to be sure of these numbers to avoid future inconveniences in the investment process.

- **Developer**: Another important thing that must be done by whoever is going to make the investment with these applications is to review the history of the company behind the home in which you want to invest. That is, review the lawsuits you had, whether you were involved in fraud or something like that. This step is very simple, as it is enough to put the name of the developer in Google and see if any of this comes out.

It should be noted that this type of investment has attractive returns, which can exceed 20% annually. However, it also has its risks, such as the department not being sold on time, which would cause the annual return to decrease or not being able to sell at the price you originally wanted.

2) Crowdfunding real estate debt

In this investment model what is done is to finance a loan that will be secured by real estate. They are very safe investments since the guarantees usually have three times the value of the borrowed silver, which makes the danger of not paying is very small. Like the previous one, there are also platforms that allow you to do this kind of crowdfunding and invest:

Briq: in Briq the amounts to invest are very low and most of the offers allow you to pay quarterly. However, investing in this platform has an annual cost of 1% over the amount of the investment.

M2CROWD: it is a good platform for this type of investment, since they have low amounts, quarterly payments and do not charge commission.

Expansive: these offers bimonthly payments and small amounts. However, they take a very long time to show the offers.

Finally, it is necessary to clarify that this type of investment is divided into two payments:

1. Periodic payments of interest: in this modality, according to the interest, they give you payments every so much time. Most commonly they are bimonthly or quarterly payments that are applied on the interest. The capital is returned once the period ends. This modality is interesting because it allows a constant flow of money.

2. Payment at the end of the period: in this mode the money is returned with the interest generated once the period is over.

Buying part of a property

In this option you can buy a property between several people. They can be friends, family, associates, etc. After investing, the rents are distributed according to what each one invested. There are platforms that allow you to do something very similar to this. One buys a percentage of a house and receives monthly rents according to what has been invested.

100 bricks: this platform offers you a list of multiple commercial properties of which one can buy a small percentage. Generally, real estate is managed by experts, which helps tenants who will be staying a long time and won't cause problems. The yield is generally around 15% per year. It is a very good opportunity if what the client is looking for is to have a constant cash inflow without many worries.

Retna: in this platform it is allowed to buy a part of the residential property, which was created with the objective of having the greatest amount of money in rents per square meter. They are usually projects with a lot of innovation. The bad thing about this platform is that the minimum amounts are much higher than the previous options, which are above 20205 dollars.

3) Investing in escrows

Escrows are a wonderful opportunity to invest in the real estate market with little money, because you can start investing with 0.40 dollars. An escrow has portfolios that makes real estate investments. Usually what you do is buy a property and rent it. The profits obtained are distributed among those who have invested. But there are also escrows that take care of developing the property. There are many different types of escrows, with different benefits and disadvantages. This is why it is important to soak up the supply of this type of investment, to see its benefits, its disadvantages, how it is managed, which market it is turning to. The good thing about this modality is that they are very liquid, which allows you to buy and sell when you want, without feeling tied for certain periods of time.

Latest news on the sale of properties in the United States

According to a lot of recent news about the U.S. real estate market, the most recent data is not very good for 2019. The National Association of Realtors (NAR) explained that contracts to buy old houses fell during November 2018, which may be a clear indication of market weakness.

> **"NAR indicated that the pending home sales index fell 0.7% at the end of November last year.** This is an indicator that analysts use to project how they expect the market to move in the next month or two months later and this fall was unexpected for many of the experts in the sector" (Real Estate America, 2019).

This fall in contracts is much better understood if we compare the values with those of November 2017, where a fall of 7.7% is observed. In addition, it should be pointed out that this value represents a large fall that has been occurring in sales in November for 11 consecutive times.

This, which is happening in the United States, gives the somewhat negative signal that pending sales were coupled with a real estate market that was constrained by mortgage rates. They are also facing a reduction in the supply of land for new construction and a lack of professional labor. All this adds up to generate a picture that ended up reducing bids on inventories of real estate available for sale.

On the other hand, you can see that in the real estate market in the United States there were not good options or opportunities for those who want to buy their first home in recent months. Most of the time, very few houses are available and those that are, most of the time, exceed the value of the budgeted young professionals, as well as the newly formed families or for many of those who hope to become owners.

> **"The price of homes rose 12.9% in Las Vegas, but so did San Francisco (11.2%), Denver (8.1%) and Boston (8%), according to** estimates by Core Logic. These were the four U.S. cities that saw their prices advance the most between October 2017 and October 2018."
> (America Real Estate, 2019)

All this that is happening on the North American continent adds up to a construction sector that is either halted or stagnant. The housing deficit is estimated at between 1 and 2 million dwellings, which clearly resulted in increased demand and reduced supply. Against this is that housing prices soar during this time, as there are more people interested in buying and fewer homes available for it.

In addition to the absence of housing offers, it adds to all this the fact that paying a mortgage is becoming increasingly difficult. Especially to those who belong to the lower classes, as well as to those who are part of the middle classes. This is because the Federal Reserve decided to implement a policy of raising interest rates as a possible solution to curb domestic inflation in the United States.

However, the real estate sector in Las Vegas, Nevada is one that has not experienced these problems. What's more, since 2008 he's not going through a better time than this. This is because a large number of Californians are arriving massively attracted by being able to get more benefits with less money, unlike in their state.

> **"Home Builders Research, for example, reported that in the first four months of this year, 22% more homes were sold in Las Vegas** than in the same period in 2017. This is driven by attractive prices around 290,000 dollars. "(America Real Estate, 2019).

Pía Ordoñez, who works in the real estate sector in Las Vegas and Henderson, explains that out of every twenty calls made to her, 50% are from clients in the state of California who wish to buy property in the area.

The agent states that there are three types of buyers who come from California: those who make the decision of their small Californian home in order to live in a large house in Las Vegas, professionals who travel constantly and prefer to be based in southern Nevada, and those who cannot obtain enough resources to own a home in California and see that it is much more profitable to invest their savings in a more affordable state. "Those who have the cash have the advantage, because they don't depend on a bank and apart from that they are willing to pay more than the appraisal says many times to be able to keep that property," Ordóñez said. "(American Real Estate, 2019).

It should be clarified that the buyers who have the greatest problems in acquiring properties are the locals, especially when it is the first time they are going to do so. So, as in all markets, as there is little supply and many buyers, the vast majority compete with each other with cash in hand.

Although we previously talked about Florida being one of the most attractive places to invest, it is also one of the most dangerous for real estate. This is due to the tropical storms that afflict the area. The effect of Hurricane Michael on properties highlighted the real estate market's concern about climate change.

Hurricanes Harvey in Houston and Maria in Puerto Rico put real estate companies to consider homes that were able to withstand category 4 hurricane winds, as well as rising sea levels. Two problems that seem to remain very common in U.S. coastal cities. Without a brake on climate change, this will become an increasingly common problem.

In Florida alone, the losses caused by Hurricane Michel on properties amount to between $2 billion and $3 billion, all caused by strong winds in Florida alone. To this must be added another $1 billion in damage caused by the cyclone surge.

In Mexico Beach, Florida only one house could withstand the winds of Hurricane Michel. Their secret was that they built it on reinforced concrete and piles. This technique could be the solution to avoid millionaire losses in the face of these hurricane winds. However, this results in house construction costs doubling for every square meter, according to a report published by The New York Times.

The U.S. real estate sector then wonders whether the problems posed by climate change will eventually force the sector to invest in reinforced housing in cities close to the sea and thus be able to improve coverage associated with rising sea levels and the frequent occurrence of tropical storms. Or if the best solution would be to move residential areas away from the coast.

Conclusion

In conclusion, there are companies like Prodigy Network or Miami Tango that accompany the client in the processes of legal and fiscal advice, as well as to administer the real estate. On the other hand, having a real estate broker is important as it allows the investor not only to obtain a good offer but also to ensure the rent and reduce the risks. Schedules also vary depending on the company offering the services. The services of companies can be ignored, but it is essential that those interested in investing be advised by specialists in the area, such as a lawyer, an accountant and a real estate agent.

It is also important to consider the following factors:

1. Analyze the property you want to buy. See if your papers are up to date, if you do not have any debts, if you the property has no problems, etc.

2. Analyze the economy of the place where the property is located. This means that it is necessary to make a small study to know if the economy is not stagnant, if the place is conducive to investment, if there is a growing economy that can bring people who want to rent and want to hire the services that the owner can offer. This factor is very important because, in a stagnant economy, a rental property does not offer the

same returns as a property in a steadily growing economy.

3. It is also important to see if in the sector where the property is located there is growth of the construction market since this generates that the property is valued, especially if they are constructions for commerce.

4. It is necessary to consider the values of the rents of the properties that are in the zone. This allows you to evaluate the profitability and expenses you are looking to have while waiting for the value of the property to increase.

Being an investor in the United States is not very difficult because any person or company that can prove that they have income or means necessary to pay for the property they want to acquire, can invest in the country. However, being a foreigner, makes it a little more difficult to obtain financing in the USA due to the fact that not all banks offer loans for foreign citizens.

Local rules for investing in the United States are an issue to consider. The seller of a property must pay a tax on the difference earned between the purchase and the sale. On the other hand, at the moment it is going to be sold, those who are foreigners, suffer a 15% withholding that after having filed the tax return is released. From then on, the payment is credited with the lien on the profit made. This whole process can take about a year.

However, this withholding does not occur if the property is in the name of a company.

Also, the best places to invest in the United States are Detroit, Miami and Manhattan. Although Brooklyn is competing with the latter, as Las Vegas is coming to light in recent times.

Finally, you can invest with little money with some platforms that can facilitate investment.

Some allow you to enter an investment with a low amount and an acceptable degree of security. The mechanism with which they work is to place a percentage of money together with other people and then have the income arrive according to the percentage that was invested in the first instance. These are the ones: Crowdfunding real estate equity, M2CROWD, Inverspot, PM2.

Crowdfunding real estate debt: In this investment model what is done is to finance a loan that is going to have as collateral a real estate. They are very safe investments since the guarantees usually have three times the value of the borrowed silver, which makes the danger of not paying is very small. As mentioned above, there are also platforms that allow you to do this kind of crowdfunding and invest: Brig, M2CROWD and Expansive.

Another way is to buy part of a property. After investing, the rents are distributed according to what each one has invested. Some are 100 bricks and Retna.

In conclusion, the most important thing for those interested in investing in real estate in the United States and anywhere in the world is to evaluate their interests and resources in order to make the decisions that best fit their investor profile.

Bibliography

Real Estate America, 2018, Climate change will be the next threat to the real estate world, accessed on October 2, 2019 at http://bienesraicesamerica.com/el-cambio-climatico-sera-la-proxima-amenaza-del-mundo-inmobiliario/

Real Estate America, 2018, Las Vegas Real Estate Market attracts more and more buyers, accessed October 2, 2019 at http://bienesraicesamerica.com/mercado-inmobiliario-de-las-vegas-atrae-cada-vez-mas-compradores/

Real estate America, 2018 a bad year for home buyers, accessed October 2, 2019 at http://bienesraicesamerica.com/2018-un-mal-ano-para-los-compradores-de-viviendas/

Real estate America, 2019, Pending sales of homes in the U.S. fell unexpectedly, accessed October 2, 2019 at http://bienesraicesamerica.com/ventas-pendientes-de-casas-en-los-eeuu-cayeron-de-forma-inesperada/

El economista, 2017, inversiones en real estate para jóvenes consulado el 2 de octubre de 2019 en https://www.eleconomista.com.mx/finanzaspe

rsonales/Inversiones-en-bienes-raices-para-jovenes-20170223-0117.html

Management, 2018, Manhattan: Real estate investors prefer Brooklyn, accessed October 2, 2019 at https://gestion.pe/mundo/eeuu/manhattan-quienes-invierten-bienes-raices-prefieren-brooklyn-247050-noticia/

Forbes, 2018, How to Invest in U.S. Real Estate, accessed October 2, 2019 at https://www.forbes.com.mx/como-invertir-en-bienes-raices-en-eua/

The new Herald, 2019, South Florida, accessed October 2, 2019 at https://www.elnuevoherald.com/noticias/sur-de-la-florida/article233289777.html

La Nación, 2018, Donde invertir en Estados Unidos, accessed October 2, 2019 at https://www.lanacion.com.ar/propiedades/donde-invertir-estados-unidos-nid2185701

Ámbito, 2018, Cinco claves para invertir en inmuebles en Estados Unidos, accessed October 2, 2019 at https://www.ambito.com/cinco-claves-invertir-inmuebles-estados-unidos-n4034087

Clarin, 2018, Doing Real Estate Business in the U.S., accessed October 2, 2019 at https://www.clarin.com/arq/hacer-negocios-inmobiliarios-ee-uu_0_HkHJDpjnz.html

Real estate America, 2019, Home sales fell 62% in Miami since the close of 2018, accessed October 2, 2019 at http://bienesraicesamerica.com/ventas-de-casas-cayeron-62-en-miami-dade-al-cierre-de-2018/

Posibles inversiones, n/f, 10 razones para invertir en el sector inmobiliario, consultado el 2 de octubre de 2019 en https://posiblesinversiones.com/invertir-en-propiedades/10-razones-para-invertir-en-el-sector-inmobiliario/

La República, 2018, Los requisitos que debe cumplir para invertir en finca real en Estados Unidos, accessed October 2, 2019 at https://www.larepublica.co/finanzas/los-requisitos-que-debe-cumplir-para-invertir-en-finca-raiz-en-estados-unidos-2771277

Cubic Meters, 2012, Tips for Investing in the United States, accessed October 2, 2019 at http://www.metroscubicos.com/articulo/consejos/2012/10/15/tips-para-invertir-en-estados-unidos